A KILL HOUSE

KU-069-210

WITHDRAWN FROM THE POETRY LIBRARY

❖

ADRIAN FOX

❖

Belfast
LAPWING

First Published by Lapwing Publications
c/o 1, Ballysillan Drive
Belfast BT14 8HQ
lapwing.poetry@ntlworld.com
http://www.freewebs.com/lapwingpoetry/

Since before 1632
The Greig sept of the MacGregor Clan
Has been printing and binding books

All Lapwing Publications are
Hand-printed and Hand-bound in Belfast
Set in Aldine 721 BT at the Winepress

ISBN 978-1-907276-32-3

CONTENTS

A KILL HOUSE

❖

ADRIAN FOX

the theory of poetry is the theory of life

Wallace Stevens

For
Rene and Dennis

life is a pigsty

Morrissey

SWIM TO ME
I.M Jeff Buckley

Through the dancing seaweed
And the debris of man with
The silent solitude of an animal
Burrowing in water, hibernating
Through the cold dark winter
You swim back to your father
Where you belong.

ODE TO THE WEEKEND

1.

Another lonely weekend looms:
It begins with crows rain and the hum
Of life out there, again. The wind picks up
And pushes the day into solitude and silence.
The squares of venetian blind are animated
By light through the sides of the curtain
They blur abstract diminished by fading light
And enfold the shadows on my ceiling into grey.
My piss-pot and my coffee cup are still life
Beside my book. The wind flutters leaves
Like animated life.

The day shines a Morse code through the curtain.
Poor Kathleen: my ex mother-in-law in hospital with cancer.
The trees are almost bare trembling loneliness.
The raindrops are blobs of transparent clarity
mirroring the majestic almighty silence
Of this cathedral, dripping tears of blue.

2.

This is an ode to my piss-pot, the bed-rail
The wheelchair and my grabber. One is
A vessel of waste but I'm going to be like
An alchemist and 'turn this muck to gold'.
The support that helps me stand rises
Like stained glass windows from my bed.

Shod in splint it takes my weight
And I fall back into my throne
And pick beauty out of this blue.

SOLITUDE

Staring into solitude
From the animal that I am
I see the colour of war
And death's debris.

This is the hell within my life.
I burrow down into my soiled earth
A miner digging gems.

There's beauty in bullet holes
And magic in bombs.
There's beauty in silence
It's dark and very deep.

I'm a miner and I capture
Essence sweet.

BLUE STONE

1.

The blue stone road has been there
Long before me or you, a smugglers route
A plot of it entombs my sister.
The lampshade reflects a nuclear symbol
On the ceiling. I'm in my cold grey bunker.
Life is like death with space.
Out there is the blue stones and the wind.

2.

My hands are as cold as death warmed up
My soul is made of poetry fluttering from
Autumn trees, branching out into summer
On a mono-chromed magpie wing.
I have to dig into the reserve of my soul
Flying through seasons to stay here not there.

A MAGIC HAND OF CHANCE
I.M John Keats

This living hand warm and cap-
        able of earnest grasping.

If it cold in a melancholic ode
In the veil of deaths delight.

When that fit of melancholy
Falls like a mournful cloud
Do not weep my rivers of tears.

HOLLYWOOD AND THE I.R.A.

You wouldn't think that once
I was a young published poet
Able-bodied in love with life.

The only books in my house
Were of Hollywood and the I.R.A.

Errol Flynn and Michael Collins
Gurued my life, I swash-buckled
Love in the clothes of war and
Even married a girl called Kitty.

ODE TO KEATS

My heart aches a numb and lonely pain
As though a sad elixir were shot through.
A pale faced melancholy rises evaporating
Rivers of sentimental happiness.

The winged leaves of nature
Sing the notes of spring, summer, autumn
And winter in instrumental ease.

It's as if at birth I was given a dose
Of negative capability and even in this death
Of life my poetic mind it is tinged with a glimmer.

Flying in this moment on wheel-chaired chariots
Like a bulb that flashes light and dark waiting
To be switched off, I feel the flowers at my feet
And the rains upon my brow embalmed in un-
adopted darkness, within this waking dream.

A SHIT SONNET

My world is coming down
With poetics and poetic literature
The meanings jump off the shelves
Pound and Eliot and all those
Cold grey words that go right over
Your head and drop like a blitz.

The war years are full of them
But it's the books in the bogs
That really matters.

All those inward outward words
That find your centre and explode
Like the real ablutions of literature.

A KILL HOUSE

Death: blood guts and brain
All pulped into a grey/white
And cured into a pudding.

A skip of swimming maggots
Above skinned coats of hide.

Pig's shot and the squeal
Cut and torn from their throats.

Dipped in a bath of scolding
Water and the layer above
Blubber shaved the parts
Hung in the window like
Decorations on hooks.

Memory hangs like a crucifix
A blood dried landscape
Aproned on a sawdust floor.

BLUES READING LOWELL

There are houses
And houses
And houses
And trees
And stains
Of rain
On cracked slabs.

Dogs and kids play
In inquisitive ditches
The flowers and the grass's
Are trampled.

We live deep
In the shadow
Of blemishes
On the paths
With the wingspan
Of a crow
On concrete.

THE BLACK HOLE POEM
For Stephen Hawkins

1.

This is the theory of everything.
Life begins like a poem.

'The source, eternity is darkness within darkness,'
The Tao Te Ching

A letter of light comes from negativity
And the universal poem is formed
Radiating light from dark
And love from hate.

2.

I woke from the darkness of a bad dream.
Why was I witnessing such darkness?
It was like a cancer or a plague.
I was afraid to go back to sleep
I lay there listening to the rain thinking
Maybe this went further back?
To Dostoyevsky or Van Gogh's time
Maybe time is timeless?
Its as if it was present at the grapes of wrath
Or in a Francis Bacon look
It feels as if I'm in the short story called 'Grief'
By Anton Chekov or on the island
Of Liam O'Flaherty's black soul.

I'm listening to the crash of thunder
like world war one or Adolf Hitler's name.
Maybe this is as Nietzche said
'I'll turn this muck to gold.'
This is the shadow of my event horizon.

EXISTENTIALIST HUMANITARIANISM

'there is but one truly serious philosophical problem and that is suicide?'

Albert Camus

The alarm went off
Vibrating another day.
I see a wheelchair
A piss-pot a bed-rail and hope.
I see beyond this room,
This hell of un-adopted kingdom.

I see a car and a life
Without this torment.
I reach down into my source
Again and plant my seeds of hope,
This is my forth year of digging my plot
And I've seen nothing grow.

I used up all my money planning a future
But god had no plans for me
I had to make my own tea, cook and clean
Unable to walk. God and the system
Let me down and I was left to dig my own hole.

I see the shoots grow
I throw back the covers and greet the day.

And that is my answer to Albert Camus.

MY BLACK ANGEL

The shadow of my wheelchair is like
A raven an Edgar Allen Poe image
Guarding my hell, my black angel.
I woke and the raven was gone
It turned back into a wheelchair,
Nature is only a footstep away
If only I could walk.

The light floods into my room
And creates a shadow of rain rippling.
They say an English-mans home is his
Castle and this hellhole is mine.
It is 2009 and I live in a middle age, limbo
All I can do is cry, I cant even commit suicide.

I've got to fit into an able-bodied timetable,
I piss in a bottle each day and wheel-
chair a wheelchair: I'm as low as a spider
Or a mouse. Wood louse and beetles highway
My floor, shell-shocked noble beasts.

The blue is crying from my eyes into
The reservoir of loss.
I've been waiting a lifetime for happiness
And four years for contentment.

I know these images come up again and again
But there's nothing else in my life only
Torment and pain. This is only half a poem
From half a man

THE ROOM

The light reflects the wheelchair
The splint and my broken door.
I'm trying to look beyond but
Everywhere I look I see disabled
Handrails and bed-rails. This is
The life from a locked-in-syndrome.
The mind flies free in a migration
But the body is a broken shell.

The only movement is the tick
And the hum of the wheelchair
Charging. The painting of tulips
Grows there in silence opposite
The man with no face. The hand
Rails are like the limbs of this room
Waiting for me to walk but this life
Is out there waiting for me to live.

THE DIMENSIONS OF A DREAM

The front back
And side view.
The elevated
Plans of a house
Or a car.
A measured
Imagined
Reality.

An arrowed space
A gear stick,
The grounds
Of a picture
Of untouchable
Quality.

BEYOND BLUE

A burnt van is lorryed
From the motorway.
Blue beyond blue
In the waiting room.

We are a bit like goldfish
Going from one side
Of the tank to the other
Or a bird or a plane
Soaring into grey.

Is this a small world
From there to here?
On the way home
On the narrow lanes
Of recovery going
Into blue beyond blue.

ROUNDABOUT C

1.

Watching a bird
Under a tree
Getting shelter
From the rain
It waddles around
Like a human
As if it owns this land.

The day is green
And grey and blue.

This poem
Is turning into a rubbing of reality
Uncovering a winged wonder in an overcast sky.

2.

Sitting in the hall at 2 a.m.
Waiting for life to stir
All I see is rain, rain, rain,
Will it ever stop raining?
Will the half built ruin
Ever be a lived in house?
The rain is getting heavier
It ripples on my path.
The streetlight throws a full-
moon hue upon the rippling rain.

The arrowed fluorescent bollard
Tells us the way to go
Left at the roundabout
And go round and round and round.

3.

Torrential rain is falling
Falling from the sky
It ripples on my path
Like galaxies reflected
From above.

'Ireland is rain, rain, rain'

Trickling down my pane
Like memories of the past
Was she there? A flash of blond
And a green carers uniform
The day is transformed
A bright sky and light on my garden.

ONLINE SHOPPING LIST

Kitchen roll
Toilet roll
Coffee
And rice
Turkey roll
Bread,
Milk
And
Cheese sliced
Nann bread
Grapes and
Cooked chicken
Twice.

RAYMOND CARVER AND ME

I dreamt that Carver was
Walking through a forest of gold
I don't know how I should interpret this
But I would say it's about the dreamer and the dream.

Carver is away off in a better place,
He has found that 'more spacious form'
So I have the earth to look forward to and wonder.

Only Carver could walk through these trees of gold
And not place a monetary value on them or weigh them
In a single metaphor but like branches of magic
Fantasy and reality coming together.

The Arabian nights meets Hubert Selby Jr
How would I interpret this?

CRAIGAVON

The sound of nature and the cars go by
We are in between a city and a town,
Plans for Spanish villas in northern Irish weather
And people from all the broken towns
Give them hope for a good year dream
A drawn out utopia sketched by pen on paper.

The balancing lakes to balance everything
Heaven to a child from the north, south,
East or west of troubled dreams.

Bringing with it all those broken dreams
Society's wasteland beyond society
But the dream comes back to bite you.

Like travellers in an unfenced reservation
Just like a trailer parked trash
OK there's alcoholics at the lakes and junkies
In the flats there's ASBO's coming out
Of the new city pre-fabbed walls
This is like an American dream gone wrong
Or a beatnik novel gone right
We're all dharma bums on nature's road.

BARCODE OF LIGHT

The sun shoots in then blinks behind cloud
The day begins like summer mornings do.
I don't know where this poem is coming from?
The reservoir of survival, a spiritual source?
No one knows I just know its magic
It gives me a purpose and just as I say purpose
The sun pierces my sight and the world
The light shines on my wheelchair and it becomes my throne.

I am the king of this un-adopted castle
Nature throws its light on my soul
And I label it Buddhist, Christian or Pagan.
You can see why civilisations have worshipped it.
It has the power of an Adidas top or a 60-inch
Plasma, I-pod or Nike brand but this trademark is free.

NOW
Turn this muck into gold

Fredrick Nietzche

I dipped into my soul
And found a well
Of negative force.

In the darkness
Within darkness
The emptiness
The loneliness
On the path of dis-
ease towards suicide.

I found what Keats called
'The negative capability'
It was not a halo
Of divine intervention
It was a tool
Of human survival.

Probably the reason
Why suicides
Are so happy
At the moment of death.

There is something beautiful
In death even spiritual
So why do people think
It depressing
When you talk of death?

When my father died
I was given a gift
I was now my whole self
I'd been given
A segment of his soul
That will live in me forever.

Maybe we don't need
An entity or a fairytale
To fall back on
For motherly love.

We have to stand
On our own two feet
Or dangle on our own two feet
And yell god is dead, I am god.

I opened the front door
And watched a bee
Dip nectar from pink petals
A bird chirp
In the distance
And two magpies of joy
In the thicket of leaves:
Green, black and white almost blue.

TIDES

The tides contour the shore,
Lapping layer upon layer
Of uncharted torn words.
Their poems searching
For a home versed in originality.

These could be the words
Of Dylan Thomas or Patrick Kavanagh
Or Robert Lowell or Sylvia Plath
Or Frost or Hughes or Keats
Or Carver: the list goes on.

This is a homage to all poets who
Have landscaped my shore
And mapped the heart and soul.
A tribute to footprints marked
In the sand, duned are the weeds
Of darkness for us to feel their light.

They are the true gods of sand and stone.

THE PATH

It's strange
How dark
Is cast by light

On

The diamond path
It comes
From sight.

KNOWING THE UNKNOWN
I.M. Wallace Stevens

Deep in the depths of irrationality
I'm being rational
Creating accidentally on purpose poetry
Like a premeditated dawn
A disabled reality.

Literature is my desire
To live in this able-bodied world.

I've been down the road of Lazarus and Berryman
Stood on the edge of my soul
Looked down at the river of poetry
But I couldn't jump
So I resign here with a blind brow.

MAHAMUDRA
for Kenneth White

'when the mind finds no place
to stop there's Mahamudra.'
                    Mahamudrapadesha

I opened the door to let a fly free
But another one came in
The vastness of grey sky
The old tree contours the wind
The stump rooted among wild, wild, wild, grass
And thistles as high as a man
Just off the diamond path that leads to my house
My un-adopted kingdom
The wheelchair slope is all marked like leaf mould
Fossils of the past drifting back from nurtured soil
The wind picks up the cars go by and nothing has to happen.

FOXHOLE

During that war
I was deep in that foxhole
In the attic wallpapered
In propaganda
On the front line
Hearing and feeling
Every bomb and bullet
As if that war was mine.

Lying here in 2009
Shooting my head out
During this pause of peace.

Thinking, what was all that for?
I'm lucky I didn't grow into a bitter man
I think there's a little
Shell-shock in my family.

Why am I still in this foxhole?

THE WRESTLER

Watching the wrestler made me realise
Just how lonely life is and was for me.
I was on those ropes motherless, family-
less and country-less but I dived into
A ring of pure poetry.

It's sad when people don't have art?
Yvor Winters the poet said, 'The artist
Whose god is art, has a religion as valid
And capable of producing great art.'

I know this film is only a fictionalised story
But it touched a raw bone and made
Me think of a versed poem I wrote
When I felt like a rat or a mouse
Or a spider, crawling into a black hole.

THE SHAPE OF SLEEP

Has moulded my pillow
Into my fathers bed
He sleeps in soil, in me
Tossing and turning memory
The few words I remember
Have fabricated sleep
And are now fabricating day.

KEATS
For Glenn and Louise

Has time stopped still?

Everything seems the same here
The piss-pot, my wheelchair, morning
The bed-rail, that line comes to mind again
Grafittied on a gable wall knocked down now
A line from a Cabaret Voltaire song:
'Why kill time when you can kill yourself'

My son is going through what I did
A threatening 'evac of the uterus'.
That future child has had a bleed like I did
So fingers crossed it stays alive.

I'll nickname it Keats after the poet
After all he formed the negative capability.
From this dark and bloody womb comes life
So any minute now the light is changing
Into a perfect day.

The leaves flutter hope and a bird flies by
Like a flag that's at full mast.
Whether this child lives or dies
Keats is in my heart.

MY PAST IS NOT MY PAST

You don't have to bring tears of loneliness.
It seems like Atilla Jozesf is still alive
I am stateless without a home.
I have been on this disabled journey
Struggling each day just to stay alive.

My past is not my past is not my past
For 45 years I've been running
Like my dad did from his bastard past.
Our lives have had a twisted melancholy
The poverty of a famined land.

Only grand canal poetry can turn this ship around
And move those locked lochs to a future
And forget those deep lochs of the past
Only we can push the tidal water
And make our father's father's father sea.

LIGHT LUNCH

These are words dancing on a page
Portraying a catalogue of Hodgkin's paintings
Under a blue moon a transparent screen
Of colour, a garden of delight.

A face I almost know along these streams of light
Rippling patios and sculptured daffodils
A light lunch, life on a plate.

A lonely spaced interior occupied by a sphere
A framed sky beside a garden of everyday lines
In a world of art in this cafeteria of people
Feeding on jealousy, gossip and hope.

Sculpted dreams in a letter of mooned memory,
Humanised movement in a hot country
Swimming in the bay of Naples
Water-falled foliage of misting vibrancy.

In a honeymoon suite, waking in another world
Beside a small good thing that transports a wreath
A glass vase and me reflected from a valley
Looking down at a Riviera or an Indian sky, fruit, rain.

A monsooned tangent in Tangiers, a splash of Paris or Italy
A lover's leap in the dark, a water-falled snapshot.
A painting reflecting these words in stilled life
Rain from a bedroom window in the evening in Scotland.

VIEW OF A PIG

Twelve throwing knives stabbed her
Before her throat was cut the squeal
Unclogged the warm blood flowed un-clotted
Her innards threw on a skip of maggots
Moving like water with an abattoir stench.

The pig lay like an open book
Her torn belly ripped, her pork chopped
Ham and rashers like leafs thumbed
By the sharpened knife, her vagina intact
His hard member thrust into her as if she
Were alive before she was tossed in a bath
Of boiling water he came as he scraped the hair
From her back:

'They're the best fucks.' he said, silent and dead.

OLDE ARDOYNE

The family boarded a plane in London
It taxied on a Belfast runway 1967.

In a taxi going through the hills of Antrim
My mother's southern view of Ireland
Quaint cottages, livestock and freedom
As if we were cycling through romantic Ireland.

The car fell from the hills through Ligoniel
Along the Crumlin Road and turned left into Ardoyne.
My father's bastard world the one he saw waking up
As an infant in a basket by a blood red door.

I woke in a Dickensian world with girls in ropes
Swinging around lampposts and boys playing
Football in the street.

My dad said there's your school it stood lonely like a prison
Surrounded by a spiked fence and a dirty red brick wall
With three layers of rusted barbed wire.

We stayed at my aunt Sarah's
A mill worker with three fingers missing,
Drab mousy hair who always wore an apron
And knelt scrubbing the front step as if waiting for god
Or some haloed man to drift into her terraced house.

I slept on a mattress on a lino floor
Looking up at a sacred heart picture
Scratching away fleas and listening
To banshees in the back alley.

A FENCED-IN POEM

I'm digging for a soul
Without god
In this wild existential
Garden.

I step away from
A sentimental path
And find light in dark
A truth in my truth.

The wind blows
Everything west
The world looks like
A Donegal landscape.

HALF-LIFE

Shadows swim in this tank.
The world outside is magnified,
A reflection in a circus mirror.

I torched the room like an explorer
Seeking treasure, as if there's still
A diamond here in the dark.

'Dolphin, my eyes have seen what my hand did.'

Basking in this lonely water
With the hard cases of silence,
Picasso shapes magnifying
The smaller dimensions of life.

A grey day watching rippling rain
A half built house
Scaffolded and abandoned
A wild, wild, wild garden.

The drip drip drip listening
To a clock tick, tick, clothes are strewn
Beside half packed boxes.

Not sure if the occupant is coming or going
The picture frames still hang and music plays
A half-life.

KIN

Cloned by modernity
Untainted by affluence
Changing a future
Into a past. Disarmed
Not Irish not English.
These words are free.

I suppose I'm lucky
My father fought
For me to write these
Words for you.

UTOPIA

A bedsit
A plot of land
Living on the dead.

A HOUSED UNIVERSE

I remember a square of tea chests
And pictures removed from walls
Love and hate, a families beginnings.

Space and tradition
Happiness and the innocence of home
Routine and treats on a Friday night,
Normality.

Outside that space was ignorance
And a confused gang who
Turned us out of our home, who burnt
It and a business to the ground.

A school assembly hall
The bonfire of Farringdon gardens
Furniture set up like a home
In chaotic normality.

Back in time further beyond
The beginnings
A scullery and a sacred heart
Picture
With an outside toilet.
Dickensian.

Inside the cave of caves
The sliding door into a dining room
A fire a dormer window
Home.

A line of tanks outside
A sniper's bullet in the window frame
Whispers of propaganda.

A cottage in a field
Nature inside the half door
Beyond the north beyond
The south beyond death
And barricades beyond the walls
Of Crumlin Road jail.

Beyond black beret's and protests
And relief in an unrelieved world
Beyond being a refugee child,
Beyond. My poetic border.

Rooms beyond a bog
The wild fields beyond
Untamed children of the 70s.
On the fringe of town
Traffic outside your door
Ruins of ramparts in the back garden.

FALL 2009

I must have been one pregnancy term
Out of the womb when Lowell commanded
The poem 'Fall 1961'. Back in time goes the
Tock-tock-tock of the plain-faced clock.

I woke to an Irish/English discord
And the linoleum smell of poverty.
I swim like a goldfish in this bowl.

Our end drifts nearer,
The moon has lifted
Radiant, beyond terror.
The able-bodied state
Is here under this glass bell.

A father's no shield
For his child.
We are like a lot of wild animals
Crying together without tears.

Nature reflects
A crow in summer
The tock-tock ticks limbo.

IRISH REPUBLICAN AFTERLIFE

Ireland you gave me the blues
And this northern gale.
You made me dig deep in my father's soil.
I write this epitaph behind you in stone:
Belfast, Dundalk and Craigavon
North and South is beyond
Interned in your special powers act
Soiled memory.

LANDSCAPE
I'd like to lean into the wind and tell myself I'm free
Townes van zandt

Leaving my room to venture out
The hall of sharp mountainous peaks
And into a domestic cave where
Rats and mice and spiders creep
Then into the valleyed living/room
Is this my disabled world?

A landscape of debris on a floor
Not unlike a war-zone from childhood
Struggling to defeat the oppressors boot
Now I just struggle to wheel-chair life
In this un-adopted landscape of wild
Grass and weeds on broken slabs.

A BALANCING POEM

The stamp of light is branded
On my ceiling like a horseshoe
Lying here at 5:46 am listening
To the wind whistle tunes through
My house. The three computer
Screens in my room are like people
Waiting for a taxi, my wheelchair.

Am I trying to normalise my life?

Its Autumn Sunday morning
The crows are out cawing just out
There beyond me like my guardian angels.
Beauty, full, black as if they had flown
From the towers of a gothic tale.
Each day I contort into my shirt
The splint on my leg and wheelchair
Into loneliness. It seems my mind
And my body are in different time-zones.

NATURE'S DAY

1.

A tent of dark envelopes the night
On this nomadic desert of arid loneliness
Duned by disability. My wheelchair
Is my camel and my piss-pot Is my flask.
Its like a bird flying overhead
My eagle of despair migrating west.

2.

I was woke by a plane going overhead
Flying so low I was waiting for another Lockerbee.
Then I heard nature sing. Strange how were ruled
By such a negative force. We live in a world full of disaster
It becomes the norm and rules our waking day.
The date is 14/10 not 9/11. If you look through history
It is full of disasters D-Day, World War One and Two
But can you hear nature.

THE SCENE

People are like raindrops
Upon a car wind screen
Washed away by wipers
To fall upon this scene.

The cry of life washed
From the womb, running
Through the alleyways
Like a gamer does in doom.

Poems aren't advice
They are moments of
Experienced life.

They are just the
Instances that held
Me here in grief.

BACKFIRE

The reflection of light
Animates the wheel chair
The splint and the broken
Door. I'm trying to look
Beyond but everywhere is
Hand rails and bed rails.
Life from locked-in-syndrome.
The mind swims in migration
But the body is a broken shell.
The only movement is the tock
Tick of the second hand and the hum
Of the wheelchair on charge.
The rails are like the limbs
Of this room waiting for me to walk
Life is out there waiting for me
To live.

The shadows of poverty fall
Like the monumental shapes
Of an old regime in a statue park.
The wars are over when you take hostage
Of your own people.

The shadows fall like distorted
Memory laying here thinking what
Was all that war about: the real I.R.A.
Need to pack that old idea in to be-
come the real I.R.A. politics is a battle
Of minds not the clash of guns. We live
On the edge of tradition and like potato pickers
In a Van Gogh or Paul Henry scene we pick
Darkness from the light.

We need minds like Nietzsche or Orwell
Conscientious objectors like Bertrand Russell
Or Robert Lowell to stop war and make people
See that these wars have been going on for cen-
       turies and we need to rewrite the book,
We are lost in tradition.

This is the first day of the rest of my life
The sun shines in and creates what the old masters
Seen in shadow creeping across the wall like a cubist
Dream.

FINDING A BALANCE

There's an arc of shadow above my head
A rainbow of darkness, a content sadness
Of lonely silence. It hangs above my head
Like the sword of Damocles. My demeanour
Is always about to cut my head off. I hear
The hum of the wheelchair charging
The gale is not out there, the storm is within.

It seems as if the world has slowed its motion
But the grass and the branches still move.
For a long time I was fuelled by drink and drugs
My head has stopped spinning.

This deep dark silence reflects of the ceiling
Like sonar pulsing light.

FORM IS THE LAST WORD

The shadow

    of a bird in flight

Drifted

    across my eyes just

Like the words

on   this   page

    Written in that moment

That display

    of thought.

Poems come like a spark

from heaven.

They need silence and solitude

To become written words

That find their own form.

A Kill House

Adrian Fox

A Kill House